ICKY WORLD

WE NEED SLIME!

By Addy Farmer
Illustrated by Scott Garrett

WAYLAND

First published in Great Britain in 2023
by Wayland

Series Editor: Grace Glendinning
Series Designer: Peter Scoulding

HB ISBN: 978 1 5263 2312 5
PB ISBN: 978 1 5263 2313 2

Printed and bound in China

Wayland, an imprint of
Hachette Children's Group
Part of Hodder and Stoughton
Carmelite House
50 Victoria Embankment
London EC4Y 0DZ

An Hachette UK Company
www.hachette.co.uk
www.hachettechildrens.co.uk

MIX
Paper from
responsible sources
FSC® C104740
FSC
www.fsc.org

The website addresses (URLs) included in this book were valid at the time
of going to press. However, it is possible that contents or addresses may
have changed since the publication of this book. No responsibility for any
such changes can be accepted by either the author or the Publisher.

CONTENTS

SLIME – the bare essentials

Mucus, sludge, goo, gloop, ooze, gunk – there are so many words for slime! But what IS it?

What IS slime?

Slime is a thick, wet substance that can come from the bodies of animals, plants and other organisms, such as slime moulds (see pages 20–21).

In this book, we'll have a look at the slimy mucus that keeps many living things healthy, from humans to slugs.

Did you know you can read this page because there is a filmy slime over your eyes to keep them from drying out?

All sizes of slime

We've all seen a slimy snail trail, but we need a microscope to spot the living slime that can spread as a thin film on the surface of glass and wood.

Slime on glass

Slime on wood

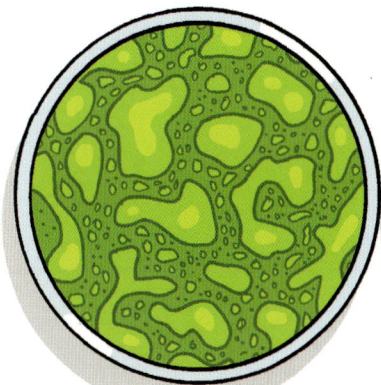

If you don't clean out your fish tank, slime grows there, too. These types of slime are usually made up of millions of microscopic microbes.

Amazing slime!

Slime has been used for important and interesting reasons throughout history – from dyeing clothes to curing illnesses.

It's time to take a deep dive into the amazing world of slime ...

In the beginning of time ...

Slimy start

Palaeobiologists are scientists who study how life on Earth got started, from the first cells to the complex life we see today. These experts think that slime has been on Earth for billions of years – and was a key stage in the formation of life on our planet.

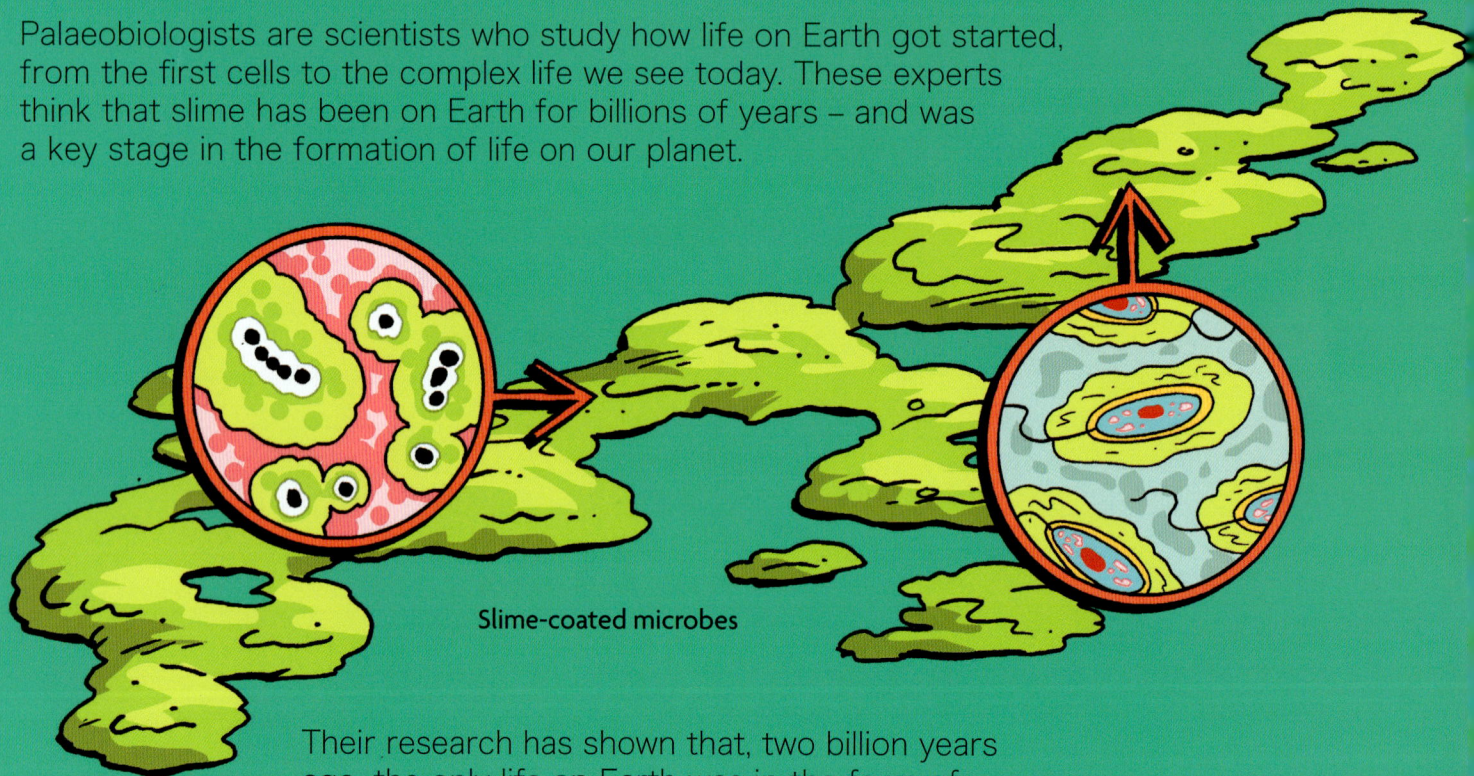

Slime-coated microbes

Their research has shown that, two billion years ago, the only life on Earth was in the form of microbes coated in slime. This microbial slime covered the seas and oceans.

The nickname for this slimy time on Earth is 'the boring billion'.

... there was SLIME

But where did all this slime come from?

Life from slime

Scientists now believe that this slimy blanket allowed life to form, or evolve, underneath it – not so boring after all!

As Earth's climate changed, the surface slime disappeared and all sorts of slimy sea creatures appeared, such as jellyfish, corals and sea anemones.

Alien slime?

Have you seen any slime in the grass around ponds? Hundreds of years ago, people thought this came from 'star bogies' that landed on Earth to start life. This 'snot' was more likely frogspawn or even the vomit of a predator who had eaten the frogspawn. Bleugh!

A close-up on slimy microbes

Let's take a closer look at the smallest slimy organisms and see how they become whole communities of slime, which are important for the health of our planet and ourselves.

Tiny slime

Microbes are so small that you need a microscope to see them. They include bacteria, viruses and microalgae.

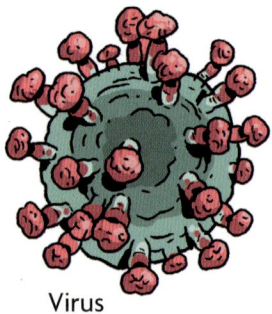

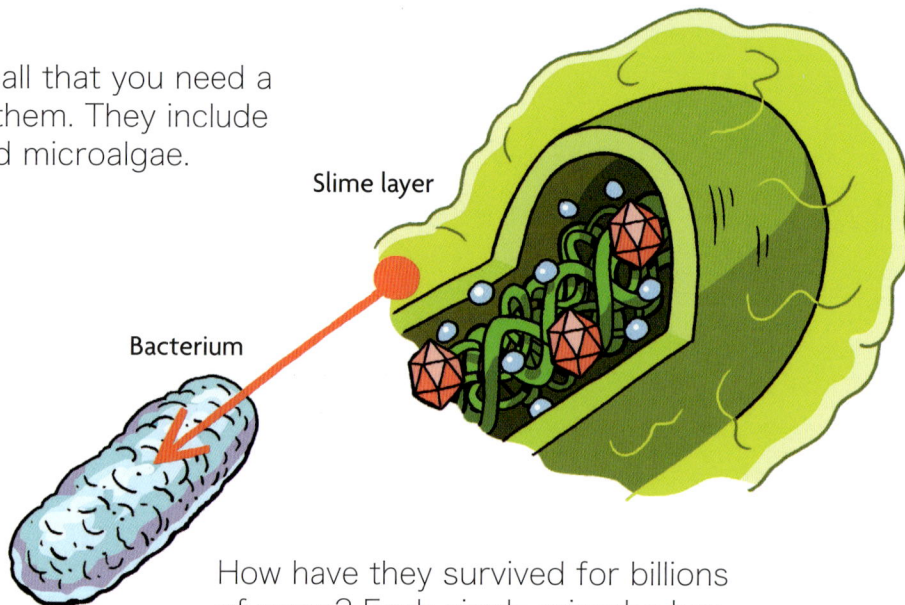

Virus

Bacterium

Slime layer

Algae cell

How have they survived for billions of years? Each single microbe has a slimy coating that protects it from the hottest sun to the coldest ice.

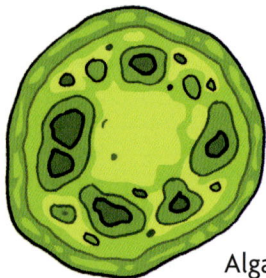

This means that slimy microbes can survive in all sorts of environment – from your body to dark caves, to possibly even Mars!

Safety in numbers

When microbes get together, they form communities called biofilms. This slimy group holds our landscapes together.

The biofilm that forms on rocks in desert areas is also known as desert varnish. It holds the sand together and helps to stop erosion.

It has also been used traditionally to create beautiful rock etchings.

Microbial goo also sticks the sand and mud together on riverbeds and the seabed.

Slimy humans?

We humans have lots of slime, too. We call it mucus.

Smooth as slime

Mucus protects and moistens the delicate membranes in your body, such as the layer coating your eyeballs. It's like oiling an engine to keep it running smoothly.

Eyes have 'blinking slime'.

The nose has the first line of mucus defense against germs.

Mucus pockets are found around the nasal cavity.

Safe with slime

Snotty mucus keeps germs, dirt, plant pollen and bacteria from getting into your lungs by trapping them in your nose. When you get a cold, your nose goes into mucus-making overdrive!

The mouth has slimy saliva for breaking down food.

What colour snot have you got?
- see-through: healthy
- white: a bit of a cold
- yellow or green: maybe an infection – your immune system is working hard!

Slick as slime

Slimy mucus also keeps things moving inside us.

When you chew food, you make slimy saliva to help you swallow. Saliva is full of enzymes that help to break down food.

Salivary glands can produce up to six cups of saliva per day.

The stomach contains strong acids to dissolve food, but it is protected by its own mucus lining.

oesophagus

Down, down travels your food: through your oesophagus, into your stomach, through your pancreas and intestines and into the toilet!

All these passages and organs are lined with slippery mucus. Without it, your food would get stuck … and so would your poo.

pancreas

small intestine

large intestine

Mucus layers protects all these organs from infection, too.

Our icky human mucus is like its own ecosystem. It helps us stay in balance and keep healthy.

Slimy land creatures

Just like humans, other animals produce icky slime, which they use in different ways.

Ever seen a slug halfway up a wall? Their slime acts like glue for climbing!

Slimy movements

So many wonderful minibeasts are absolutely covered in slime.

As **slugs** and **snails** move along the ground, their slime helps protect their one big foot from sharp objects.

Earthworms move smoothly through the soil because of their slimy bodies.

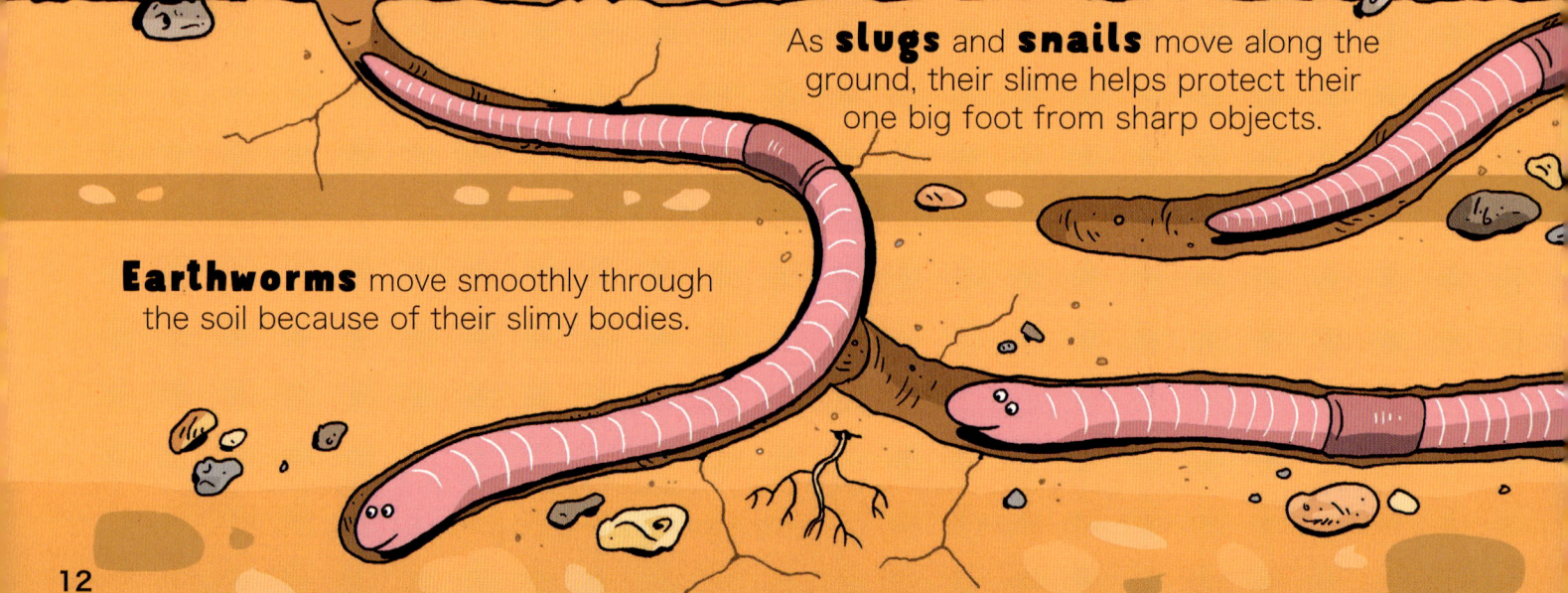

Slimy message: stay away!

The **hyena** secretes 'hyena butter' slime and rubs its bottom on trees to mark its territory. Gross, but effective!

The **hedgehog** might have lots of spines, but it still needs slime to protect itself from predators.

It makes a slippery, stinky slime from its own saliva and covers its body in it. Predators then can't sniff the hedgehog out, or maybe they don't want to!

Slimy weapons

Banana slug slime is full of special chemicals, which give any predator a numb tongue as they try to chow down. Bleugh!

The **velvet worm** captures prey by squirting a quick-hardening slime over it. The velvet worm then eats its meal, slime and all, so no nutritious slime is wasted!

Slime between land and sea

Amphibians need to keep moist to stay alive. Skin slime is all-important to their health and survival.

Fabulous frog slime

A **bullfrog's** skin slime helps prevent some bacterial and fungal infections.

Poison dart frogs live on the forest floor, where they could be easily eaten. But their slime is a poweful poison and protects them against predators!

Australian water-holding frogs have adapted to live in the desert. They bury themselves underground and mix their slime with sand. This hardens into a 'skin bag', which holds in the frogs' moisture until it rains again.

More amphibian slime uses

The **hellbender salamander**, also called a **snot otter**, lives in the water but has no gills. It uses its slimy skin to breathe by absorbing oxygen straight from the water.

Natterjack toads produce slimy secretions to keep moist in their sandy burrows. But their slime is also poisonous to put off predators!

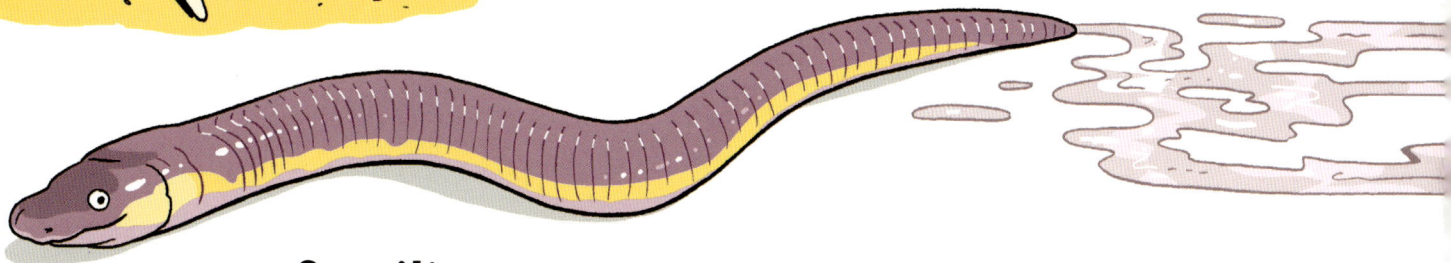

Caecilians look like snakes or worms. Their heads produce slimy mucus for crawling through the soil, while their tails sometimes secrete poisonous slime to keep predators from following.

Clever skin

Amphibians' slimy skins are very sensitive to changes in their environments. If we watch amphibians carefully, we can quickly spot ecosystem problems and act to fix them before it's too late!

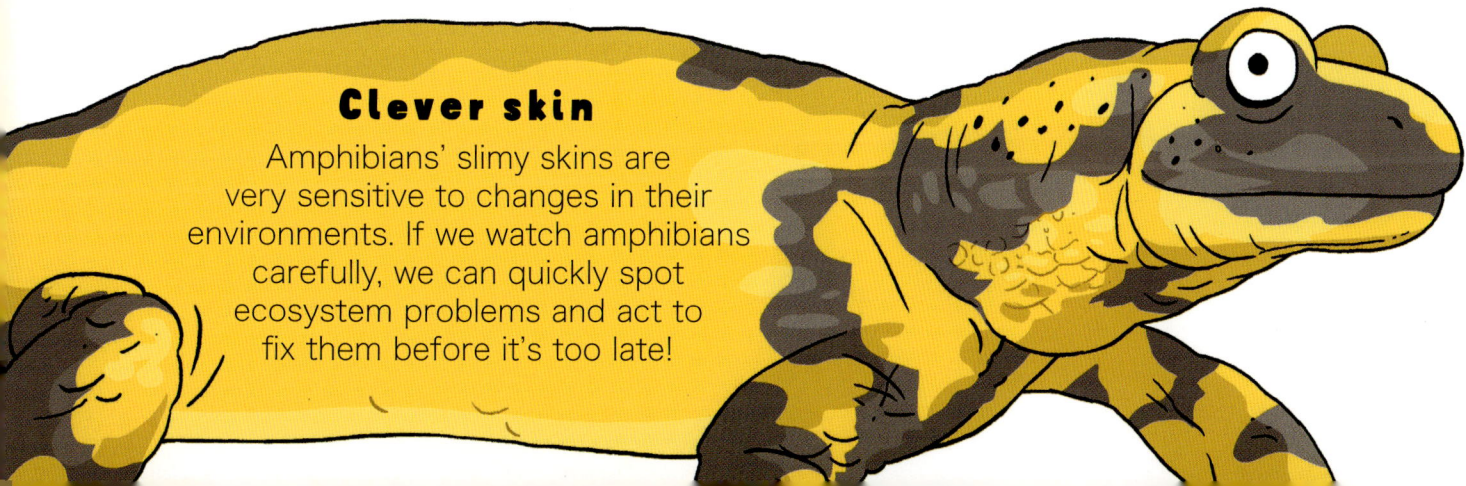

slimy sea creatures

Animals that live underwater are not going to dry out in a hurry, but they still need slime to survive.

Slime sleeping bag

Slime on all fish helps keep their gills clean and healthy. The **parrotfish** goes one step further.

This amazing animal burps out a mucus sac to sleep in every night to keep its skin free from pesky parasites.

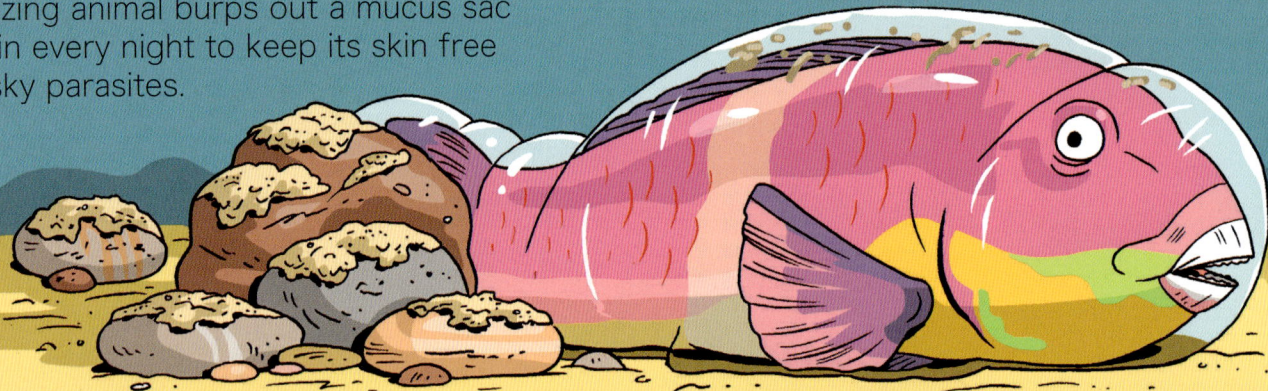

Slime palace

Giant larvaceans are almost see-through. They use their mucus to make snot houses around them, to keep safe and gather food.

Empty larvacean houses sink and become slimy-but-healthy food for animals living on the sea floor.

← Up to 1 m wide! →

Extreme sea slimers

The tiny **pearlfish** secretes slime so that it can move into a sea cucumber's bum! The slime also acts as a barrier against the toxin the poor old sea cucumber makes to try and get rid of its invader.

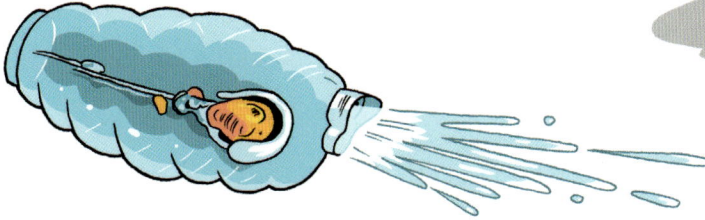

Mucus nets inside the tiny **salp** help it to filter its food out of the water. The salp then squirts the unwanted water out of its bottom.

The **lettuce sea slug** is one of nature's slimy cleaners because it feeds on tiny (also slimy) algae.

Slimy winner!

The prize for the most slime goes to the extraordinary **hagfish**, which can jet out a whole litre of snot to slip away from predators!

Hagfish (also called **snotties**) can choke their predators with gill-clogging slime.

17

Plant slime

Like animals, plants need some sort of slime to survive.

Plants have a special slime called mucilage, which is thick and gluey. They use it for all kinds of purposes.

Slime = seed spreading

When you are rooted to the ground, you need to find ways of spreading your seeds to make new plants.

Enter: the **squirting cucumber**. When its fruit is ripe, the mucilage-covered seeds are spread out with a slimy explosion.

Slimy plant seeds also travel inside animals. For example:

Bird eats delicious, sweet, seedy fruit.

Bird flies away.

Bird urgently needs a poo to get rid of the slippery seeds!

Seeds are scattered far and wide.

Slime = digestion

Many meat-eating plants use their slime to feed. **Pitcher plants'** slimy pools trap and digest insects and larger animals, such as birds and mice.

The super-sticky **sundew** plant's sweet nectar tempts flies in for a snack. The flies get stuck and the leaves begin to curl around them. Digestive juices mix with the slime and lunch is ready!

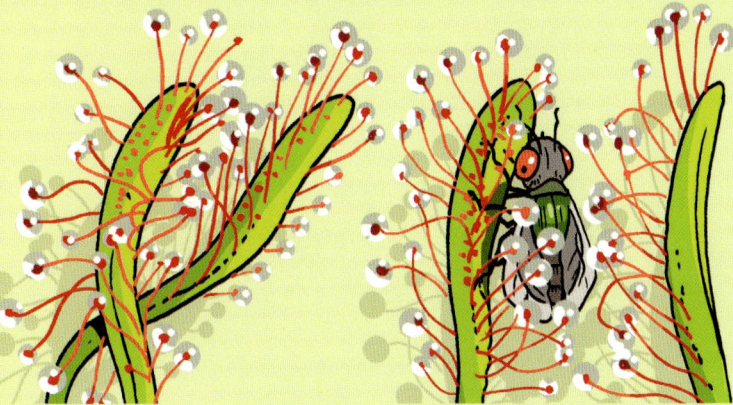

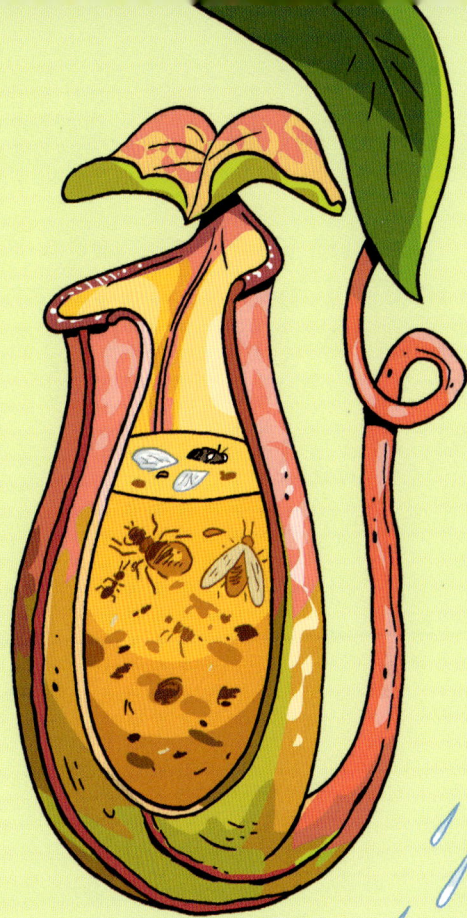

Slime = hydration

Chia seeds use slime to adapt to the heat. As soon as water hits them, they absorb lots of it and fast! This forms a coating of mucilage around each seed – good for storing water or hitching a ride on an animal.

Slime = delicious!

Humans use chia seeds' icky-sticky adaptation in cooking – to thicken sauces, as an egg replacement and to make sugar-free jam.

Slime moulds

Slime moulds are special. They look like a fungus but can move around, a bit like an animal.

Coming together

Slime moulds begin life as single cells that move around in the soil. When they run out of food, they join together to look like a slimy blob.

One common slime mould has a form you might call the 'see-through, faceless slug' stage!

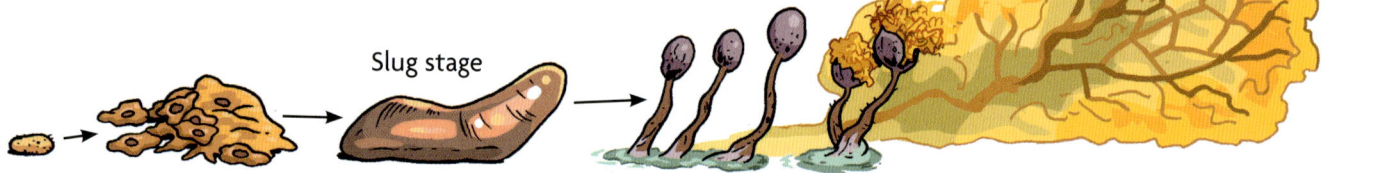

Slug stage

So many slime moulds

There are at least 900 different species of slime mould, all in different shapes and colours.

Some of them might sound tasty, but you do not want to eat them – they only share an *appearance* with their namesakes!

Black pearl

Cauliflower

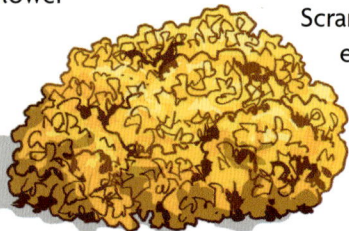

Scrambled egg

Coral

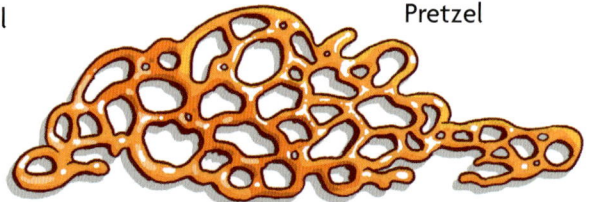
Pretzel

Slimy recyclers

Slime moulds have been on Earth for around 380 billion years, clearing and recycling.

In woodlands, they feast on rotting wood and leaves. They break down the dead stuff, which clears the way for new life.

Underwater, slime moulds called 'slime nets' play an important role in the decomposition of dead plants and animals, too.

Slow and steady slime

These amazing organisms are always on the move but very, very slowly – searching for food in the form of bacteria.

Incredibly, these brainless blobs can always find the quickest path to their food, taking the shortest route, when given a choice!

Many-headed slime mould

Inspiring slime

Slime in nature has inspired some fascinating legends, trends and science learning!

Slime stories

In Scandinavia, the dog sick slime mould was thought to be the vomit of the mysterious 'troll cat'.

In the UK, it is often called fairy butter ... or witch's butter to some.

Some of the first thriller books ever written were based around creatures emerging from slime. Even today, who hasn't seen a film where a mystery involves some sort of oozing slime?

Slimy entertainment

Slime is also something we can make and play with – inspired by the incredible natural slimes that are part of so many ecosystems!

Play-slime is a **non-Newtonian fluid**, which means that it can feel like a solid when you squeeze it, but it becomes liquidy when you let your hand go loose.

It takes the shape of whatever is holding it and is great fun!

Slime in space

Astronauts took slime moulds to the International Space Station. The idea was to inspire interest in slime and the environment – to grab the attention of the scientists of the future.

Slime has been the key to learning about our planet. And, if microbes on Mars are slime-covered, then perhaps the future of space travel is slime-covered, too ...

23

Slimy algae helping others

There are many different sorts of slimy algae and they are all important for keeping our planet in balance.

Clean air through slime

Like plants, algae get their nutrients through photosynthesis. This process releases oxygen for us to breathe. Algae are an enormous part of keeping Earth's air healthy.

Colourful slime

Microalgae give corals many of their bright colours. They live as a community on the coral, acting as coral cleaners and feeders at the same time.

They also take in coral waste, such as carbon dioxide, and give out oxygen. It's a win-win relationship called symbiosis.

There are even slimy ice algae in the sea ice around the Arctic and Antarctic!

Double-time slime

Giant kelp are large algae that also provide a home for slimy microbes and many other living things.

The slimy leaves, called blades, create shelter for fish, snails, otters, anemones and many more. All these things together make up a balanced (and slimy) underwater forest ecosystem.

Multi-purpose slime

Slimy algae can also be transformed into fertilisers or added to foods – they are full of nutrition.

Scientists also work to use slimy algae to make biofuels. These could replace fossil fuels, which contribute to climate change. Go, slime!

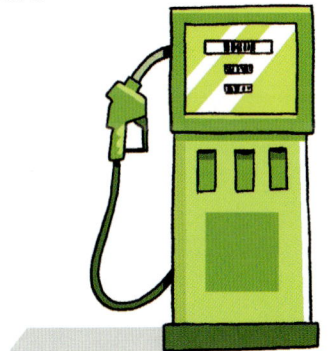

Useful partners ...

**All sorts of slimes have proved
to be useful to humans ...**

Slugs, toads and plants, saving lives!

Slug slime inspired scientists to create a sticky
but flexible glue for sticking wounds together.

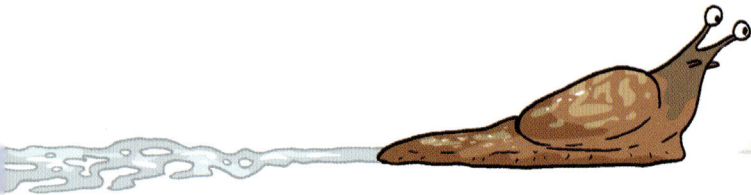

Biomedical researchers
have found that the
**Colorado river
toad's** slime can make
a medicine to help with
mental wellness.

The mucilage in
aloe plants has been
used throughout history
to treat burns and soothe
skin conditions.

... in SLIME

... and will be super important for building a sustainable future.

Sustainable slime

We can look to nature to inspire sustainable products to replace current products that hurt our environment.

The **hagfish** (above) produces buckets of quick-hardening slime (see page 17). This strong slime can be recreated in a laboratory to make strong ropes or even bulletproof vests. The slime fibres are much more eco-friendly than using products such as oil to create plastic.

Cleaning with slime

Slimy mucus acts as a filter for bacteria, so why not for filtering pollution?

Scientists are investigating **jellyfish** mucus as a biofilter for all the microplastics clogging the planet's seas and oceans.

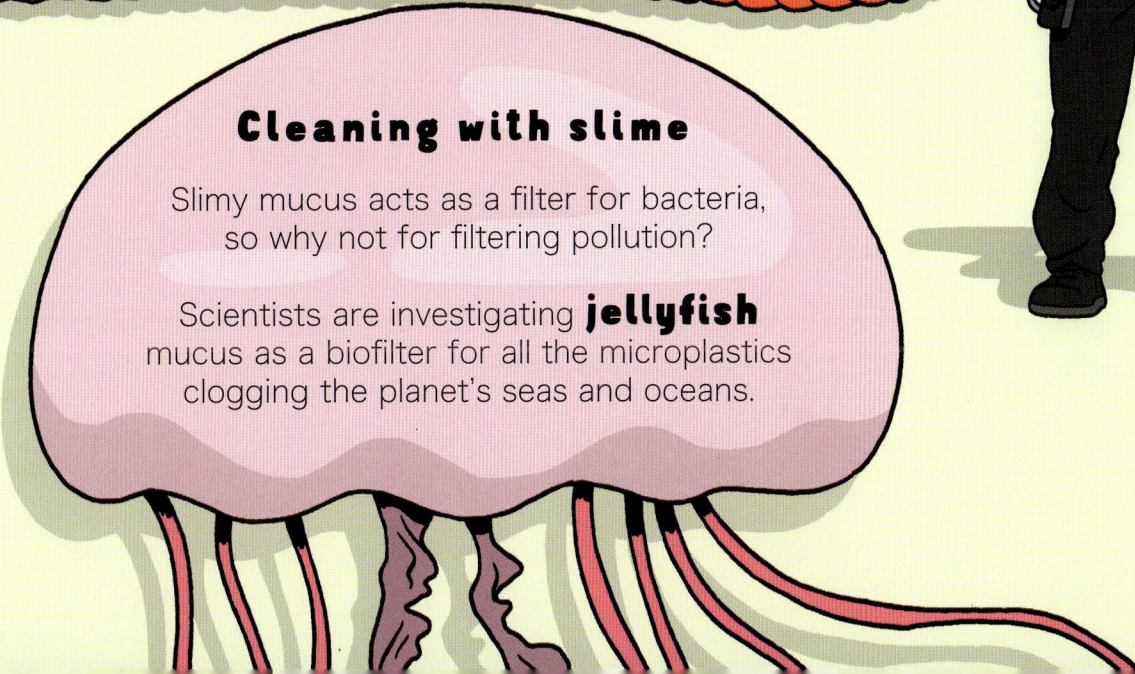

SAVE THE SLIME!

What can you do to preserve different sources of wonderful slime on Earth? CAREFUL! Leave everything safe and in its natural habitat.

Let the toads roam

Save your local slimy amphibians! Do you know of a toad crossing in your area? If not, see if you can work with your school or family to help introduce one.

Count those toads

Your community could also form a Toad Patrol. Patrol groups keep track of roads that toads cross to reach ponds in the spring.

The patrol sorts out a safe plan to count how many toads use the road during a certain time. This information helps scientists to understand how healthy your local amphibian population is.

Inform and inspire

Along with some friends and a trusted adult, head out on a slime-mould safari. They really are all around – you won't believe how many you can spot in a wet, healthy woodland.

Getting to know more about slime in your local area means that you can inform others and inspire more slime protectors.

WARNING: never disturb or touch the slime!

Your group could also go to the beach for a rockpool safari. **Careful as you go: slime is slippery!**

Make a note of the slime you find. Head to a library or use the Internet (with adult help and permission) to research your slime further. Report back to a parent, carer or teacher about your findings – knowledge is power!

29

Glossary

Amphibians – cold-blooded vertebrates (a vertebrate has a backbone) that don't have scales. Amphibians live part of their lives in water and part on land.

Bacteria – living things made of just one cell. Some bacteria cause illnesses, but others are important parts of healthy ecosystems.

Biodiversity – all the variety of life, whether that's plants, animals, fungi or microorganisms, as well as the ecosystems they form and the habitats in which they live.

Biofilter – a natural tool for cleaning air, water or other polluted substances.

Biofuel – a type of eco-friendly fuel made from, for example, plant, algae or animal waste.

Carbon dioxide – a gas found in the air, which plants absorb during photosynthesis (how they make their own food).

Climate change (or global warming) – the process of our planet heating up and our world weather changing. This is due to many reasons, including too much carbon dioxide escaping into the atmosphere. For example, carbon is released when humans clear land of plants so that they can build or mine.

Ecosystem – all the living things in a certain area and how they form a natural community.

Enzyme – a substance inside living things that acts to speed up chemical reactions in cells.

Erosion – is the gradual wearing away of rock, soil or sand by, for example, wind or water.

Etching – an art form that involves cutting a pattern or picture into a hard surface.

Fossil fuels – natural fuels, such as coal and oil, made from the remains of plants and animals that died a very long time ago.

Membrane – a very thin layer of cells that act as a barrier or lining.

Microbes – the tiny living microorganisms you cannot see with the naked eye, for example bacteria and viruses.

Microalgae – plant-like living things that can make food from sunlight through photosynthesis.

Parasite – a living thing that lives in or on another living thing of a different species (the 'host'), and gets its nutrients from the host's body.

Photosynthesis – the process in which green plants use sunlight to make their own food. Photosynthesis is necessary for life on Earth.

Viruses – a microscopic living thing that infects other living things.

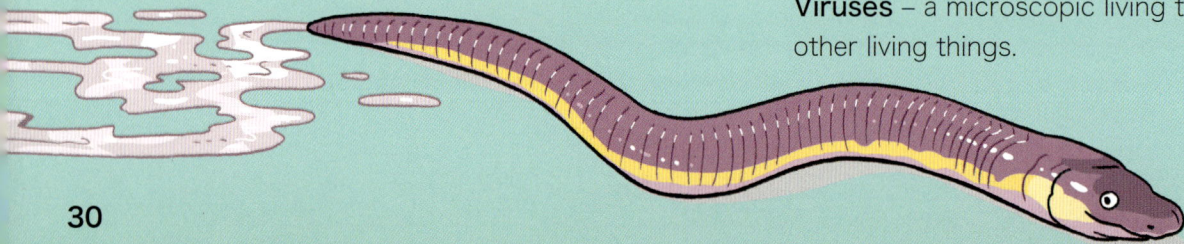

Further info

Find out more about the icky bits of nature!

Books:

The *Animals Do* series
by Paul Mason, Tony De Saulles & Gemma Hastilow, Wayland 2018–20
The Poo That Animals Do, *The Wee That Animals Pee*
The Farts That Animals Parp, *The Snot That Animals Have Got*

The Poo-niverse
by Paul Mason and Fran Bueno, Wayland 2020

The *Outdoor Science* series
by Sonya Newland & Izzi Howell, Wayland 2018–19

Websites:
Check out this website for slime mould identification:
www.naturespot.org.uk/gallery/slime-moulds

Find your nearest toad crossing if you live in the UK:
www.froglife.org/what-we-do/toads-on-roads/tormap/

Biofilms as art in photography:
www.biofilms.ac.uk/biofilm-image-gallery/

INDEX